"But I Can't Afford To Save"
Simple Strategies to Start Building Prosperity

R. Lee Townsend

Real Town Publishing

© 2021 R. Lee Townsend

All rights reserved.

The characters and events portrayed in this book are fictitious. Any similarity to real persons, living or dead, is coincidental and not intended by the author.

No part of this book may be reproduced, or stored in a retrieval system, or transmitted in any form or by any means, electronic, mechanical, photocopying, recording, or otherwise, without express written permission of the Publisher.

ISBN: 9798538988266

Printed in the United States of America

July 2021

the first of many --

for J

Table of Contents

Foreword 8

    The Lean Years 9

    The Beginnings Of Relative Prosperity 11

    Feast Or Famine 13

    The Light At The End Of The Tunnel 16

1 - Personal Discipline - Commitment to Consistency 18

    Make The Commitment 18

    The Biggest Danger In Slipping On Your Commitment 20

    A Few Early Tips 22

2 - Pay Yourself First 24

    Balance What's Coming In And Going Out ... 24

    So How Much Do I Pay Myself? 25

    Drastic Measures 26

    More Economizing Tips 27

    Bag It 28

    Don't Buy Food Just To Rot 29

- Sharpen Your Culinary Skills 30
- Save Dining Out For Special Occasions Only 31

3 - Even More Economizing Tips 33
- What Do We Want vs. What Do We Need? 33
- The Life Of Your Car 34
- Miserly or Frugal? 36

4 - The "Coffee Can" Saving Method 37
- Drawing The Line 38

5 - Easy Credit Ain't All That Easy. 39
- Credit Card Trap 41

6 - Live In Your Savings Account 45
- What Is A Mortgage? 45
- Who Owns Whom? 46
- The Game Isn't Over For Renters 48

7 - Build A Buffer 50
- Not The End Game 51

8 - Taking Charge 52
- Quantum Schmuantum - Throw Out Wishful Thinking 52

- When Leveraging Can Be Beneficial 54
- 9 – Invest and Diversify 57
  - Opening An Investment Account Is Easy 58
  - Diversify 59
  - Deal With Stock Market Downturns 60
  - When Do I Divest? 62
  - Cryptocurrency 63
- 10 – Go Rogue 66
  - What Is Your Skillset? 67
  - Make A List, Keep Checking Twice (and More) 70
  - Keep Your Promises 70
  - When You Get Paid 71
- 11 – My Way Of Tracking Finances 72
  - It Works For Me! 72
  - Start Simply 74
  - Not My Way Or The Highway 74
- 12 – Conclusion 81
  - Be Committed 81
  - Turn The Negative Around 82

Gear Yourself To Delayed Gratification 82

Watch The Big Picture, Some Parting Thoughts 83

ABOUT THE AUTHOR...85

Foreword

"But I can't afford to save any money, there's nothing left over after most of my bills are paid. I'm constantly having to rob Peter to pay Paul just to get by." Has this, or something like it, been your response to the advice that was ever offered to you, when some well-meaning friend, family member, or financial guru tells you to "Pay yourself first?"

"But I can't afford to save" are certainly words I have spoken in the past. I thought, "It's easy for them to blithely say, those folks who have suggested doing such a thing are not walking in my shoes. What does 'Pay yourself first' even mean? I'm barely scraping by right now, all of these other people and institutions are already getting all of my money. If I pay myself first, I won't be able to make my bills."

Hogwash.

This is the typical rationalization for those who live paycheck to paycheck, day to day enduring more financial crises than are necessary. It's not a valid excuse at all. What they don't realize is what they're actually doing is creating financial crises for themselves.

This mindset is a tell-tale signal that we have not learned good money handling skills, neither through our upbringing nor from educational institutions. And we really cannot dismissively blame our upbringing, because our "upbringers" may have never known how to implement good financial planning in the first place, because they never learned it. Here they'll get a pass.

The conspiracy theorist in me might say that our educational system is designed to teach you basic arithmetic, sure, but neglects to tell you how to implement it effectively and practically in your personal financial life. They will only provide you with enough information in order to become a good worker. After all, the public educational institutions are funded by big government, which is controlled by big business, and their joint aim is to keep the masses under control. The robber-barons of yore still exist.

It's an extreme viewpoint, sure, but there are always seeds of truth in any conspiracy theory. Fortunately, real-life is not quite as completely nefarious as the paranoia of my inner conspiracy theorist would suggest.

The Lean Years

Career-wise, I started out as a professional musician, and let me tell you, when you're starting a career in such a high risk, highly competitive business, you start your journey at the very lowest rung of the financial ladder. In the '70s I played music in a band, and lived in a communal setting with my bandmates. For several years we each drew a pay of anywhere between $40 and $90 per week to live. Thank goodness for some diehard fans, who prevented us from starving, quite literally. More than just coming together onstage to make music, out of necessity we had to live together, at times with as many as 14 of us living in a single rental house. To plagiarizingly paraphrase, they were the best and worst of times. We were a steady working musical group, though.

We worked hard, but not smart. All of the money for the rental of our communal house was paid for off the top, as well as the other business expenses (equipment, agent/management commissions, crew, maintenance, gas to get to transport the gear to the gigs, etc.). We divided up what was left over to cover personal food, insurance, our vehicles and in general anything not related to the music business. We squeaked by, but just barely, and set aside whatever pittance we could so we could occasionally pay for a recording studio to go in and make demos of our original music.

We worked all the time back in those days, but for not much money while getting established. We took just about any gigs that came our way, no matter the compensation, even to the point of acccpting union jobs at state hospitals and prisons, where we'd be paid $9 per hour each to play music.

Saving money for us individually in those days was unthinkable.

Because of continuously living on the razor's edge, It affected each of us in the group pretty severely whenever we would lose a gig due to a snow cancellation, or incur that extra expense of having our truck towed to the gig because of engine problems. Yes, it really happened; and not just a couple of times either.

We had no buffer saved to mitigate these occasional little inconveniences. The effect that one lost gig had on our already precarious situation would easily financially set us back for three months, or more. Yes, we survived it, just barely, through all of those years. Our survival was mostly at the benevolent hand of Providence itself, I'm certain.

The Beginnings Of Relative Prosperity

When I turned forty some years later I was raising a family and began to wise up. I realized that I had nothing saved, no promise for any semblance of comfortable retirement years. So I went out and got a "real job" in what I refer to as the old musician's boneyard: the commercial audio visual industry. I still kept my hand in music, though. I had invested so much time and effort into it, and wasn't ready to toss it all aside. But I also needed to start looking at my future and begin earning a decent living for my growing family.

So then I began again at 40 into an entry level job, and over the next 25 years worked my way up to senior design engineer and control systems programmer, was constantly learning and training, and my salary had eventually blossomed to just over six figures.

I've had my ups and downs over the years, but thankfully my overall quality of life improved. I had started a 401k retirement fund, later to be converted to IRAs, and was working hard to pay off a mortgage. But never really managed to squirrel away much extra cash; I put most of it into my home. Then a divorce followed, and I became emotionally and financially wiped out.

I had to start building my life completely over again. Life savings all but wiped out, I moved back to my hometown and got a job, still in the A/V industry, and living near Baltimore, but commuting to Washington DC daily. I was in the process of gradually rebuilding my life when a huge corporate downsizing in 2012 left me laid off and out of work. The company I worked for was one of the largest in the country. They decided, for better or worse, to resort to hiring subcontractors for all of their production work, and focused solely on generating sales as their new and improved business model. Their subcontractors would do all the heavy lifting. Being a subcontractor then ended up being me.

I had built a fairly decent reputation in the industry, and there were no hard feelings in the layoff, it was just a smart business decision that I would have probably made myself had I been the employer. The company was hemorrhaging cash and change quickly needed to occur. After all, I was one of the oldest on the team, the shortest tenured, and among the highest paid.

I then went into business for myself providing contract services, both for the company that had laid me off and for many of their subcontracting vendors.

Everything was going very well at first, it was just me and I was generating about $15,000 per month by my second month in business. Things were looking up. I had secured a federal subcontract design job in Germany for a week in January of 2013, with plans to return for the entire month of April to be on hand for the actual construction. I was traveling a lot at that time; in fact I was working on a job at USC in Los Angeles when the call came to be in Stuttgart Germany the following Monday.

The day I returned home from a week in Germany was the day the 2013 federal sequestration hit. Most of the subcontract work I was doing was for federal jobs, which suddenly went barren. I instantly went from comfortable and upwardly mobile to scrambling again. My phone did not ring for six weeks. I had a blank work calendar at that time. The return trip to Germany for the month of April had evaporated because the money for that project had been reallocated.

Feast Or Famine

We who have not grown up having been taught good money management practices tend to live in the "feast or famine" mindset. For us there's a propensity to use that "I can't afford to save" mentality in the lean times, conversely in the good times the cash seems to have a tendency to roll out the door just as quickly as it comes in. In those times there's no panic, no urgency and we allow our already-meager money management skills to lapse.

We just throw our extra money at our problems to make them go away. But what happens when the source of the extra money goes away? I was writing the checks, but wasn't minding the store.

Not wanting to get caught in the same paralyzing setback condition I had endured in my music days, I first started to figure it out and began using the tips that are contained in this book. I had to get serious about my personal finances, and only squeaked by doing odd jobs as I could locate them.

After six weeks of panic the phone did ring, and it was from an employment headhunter. I interviewed for a position with a company located 22 minutes from my home and negotiated a high 5-figure salary. Ironically, after I interviewed and before I started working for the new company, my phone started regularly ringing again with new contract work. But I had already decided to go back to the corporate route, closed up shop and again became a corporate employee. I was determined that I didn't want to get caught in those financial straits again.

I worked for a very progressive company for the next seven years and eventually crossed that annual six-figure threshold. The company was growing, it had more than doubled in size while I was there and was continually expanding.

I again began the trek on the road to my financial recovery and started with simply keeping a rudimentary pro-forma ledger. What's coming in, what's going out, and running balances on everything, projected through the end of the year. It was an annual financial plan in ledger form which became the dynamic instrument of my financial security. I created spreadsheets for my checking accounts, savings account, investment accounts (what remained of my then-IRA after the divorce), and projected my reasonable expectations into the future for the entire year. They were loose, but historically fact-based expectations of what would be coming in and what would be going out. I'll explain in more detail later in this book.

The new system I started using had begun to work, but as soon as I had started saving a modest amount of money, the discipline of keeping up with the daily tracking began to fade. I found myself "too busy" at work to keep up with it. And I soon found myself in the same money-in, money-out situation. More cash was at stake, and with the same net results as before.

That's the trouble spot we can easily get ourselves into: when things are going well, we tend to think that our new age of prosperity will never end. I began to wonder again why I wasn't financially moving forward, despite the fact that I was making more money than I ever had, well above the national norm for a typical worker-bee. But my spending was way out of line. So I started tracking my finances again, and re-adopted the "pay myself first" attitude. It was beginning to work; I finally started saving money again, managing to set aside a couple thousand dollars in savings in a relatively short time.

Then the pandemic hit, and life as we knew it shut down.

During the last week of March 2020 I was quarantined pending the results of a Covid-19 test. I had potentially been exposed, and I was working from home. My supervisor set up a teleconference meeting. On the phone was my supervisor, our division leader, and our HR manager. I was again blindsided and laid off in another corporate downsizing, but also again in good standing with the company, and with the possibility of future rehire. They had let go a large portion of their tech staff that day, ironically on April Fool's Day. It was not until the following Friday that I received my negative Covid test results.

For others, returning to work after the pandemic shutdown downsizing was a viable option. For me, though, I was then two months shy of my 65th birthday. So I reluctantly elected to retire. I started receiving Social Security in June 2020 and had lived off of my nominal severance package since my termination. My income dropped to less than a quarter of my original earnings in an instant.

Unfortunately my regular bills did not follow suit.

Since I had been only newly re-committed to tracking my personal finances I only had enough saved to sustain my living expenses for one month or so; that paltry couple of thousand that I had socked away would only cover me for a very short while. I collected unemployment to get by and sought other work, but at the time everyone in my field was under a hiring freeze. And even with collecting unemployment, it still was not equal to what I was earning before. Not anywhere near. I was in a pickle and under the gun (bet you never heard that sentence before, sorry for the mixed metaphor).

I then started doing odd delivery jobs to make ends meet, on my own schedule. Even so, I was generating considerably less than I was previously, I re-committed to a formal financial discipline and adopted the steps contained later in this book, and have actually been able to save enough money to be able to sustain me for quite some time. I won't be vacationing on the Riviera anytime soon, but neither will I go hungry nor homeless, and am in a position to withstand just about any even the slightest bumps on the track, that in the past would've easily derailed me.

The Light At The End Of The Tunnel

There are two significant ways of living more comfortably in the short term: earn more or spend less, or a combination of the two. Longer term prosperity requires consistently applying the good practices and discipline learned from working the shorter term solutions.

This book does not contain any easy get-rich-quick schemes and certainly no revolutionary ideas, just plain old common sense. Bear in mind that I'm not a professional financial advisor, far from it, this is just what works for me. It is my most fervent hope that sharing these ideas here will help you to do more than just get by, to be cognizant enough of the issues at hand in order to eventually prosper. I'm by no means rich, but I am comfortable, and am able to live very modestly and still miraculously able to set aside money for savings and investment.

Consider this as more of a guide to adopting a mindset of prosperity, and tending your financial store. There are many paths to getting yourself financially stabilized before you build or rebuild your economic empires. These are the basics.

The more you do it, the easier it becomes. Commit to it and stick with it. You'll see. The sticking with it, the conscious and consistent effort is what carries the day. It can only be accomplished by making it all habitual.

If someone like me can do it, so can you.

1 - Personal Discipline - Commitment to Consistency

This is not as bad as it sounds; it's not a prison life-sentence. Put quite simply, you'll need to consistently begin tracking everything that financially comes in and goes out. No matter which method you use, pencil, spreadsheet, database, app, dry beans in a can, or other, all it takes is a little applied thought and setup for a few hours to get started. Make it part of your DNA that this is your new culture, day in and day out, your new normal.

Make The Commitment

Once your snapshot has been brought into focus, and you can begin to honestly and realistically see where you presently financially stand, then comes the hardest part of all: making the commitment to consistently keep up with a plan to make your life better. It only works when you make these new habits a part of your entire life culture. It's where most people, including my past self, have failed. We have a tendency to, once we start building a little bit of cash savings, slack off on our financial plan.

We cannot let complacency rule the day. After all, that's how we get in this mess to begin with, right? We have to be continually and literally minding our own business, especially so in times of financial ease. You might not think that's the case, but it actually is. Financial ease is when we're most at risk for lapsing in our financial management skills, because we're not in "famine" crisis mode in those times. Like famine, feast is only a temporary thing; it can and does dynamically turn on you in a flash, just as a windfall also quickly dries up.

You need to seal the deal with yourself, and make and keep the commitment to updating your financial tracking, a snapshot of where you stand, every day or so. Admittedly, I have some days that I don't keep up for one reason or another, but I never go more than falling three days behind; any more than that makes recreating the past too much of a chore. It's best to not let yourself fall behind, but if you do find yourself beginning to slip, rectify it immediately and re-affirm your resolve.

Let me restate that: If you do find yourself slacking off, invest the time in getting caught up. In the process, remind yourself to keep it up daily; constantly remind yourself you don't want to end up in those panic situations like you did in the past. It's really not a huge deal to fit in the few minutes a day that it takes from your schedule. Sure, it can get boring, but it is necessary to keep plugging the leaks in your financial boat.

I've adopted the routine of updating my ledger the first thing in the morning, while having my morning coffee. It normally only takes a few minutes. I do all of my tracking on spreadsheets on my PC, and do most of my banking online. It simplifies the process and minimizes the number of outstanding checks that I need to track. I log on with my bank and investment company, check on my accounts, transfer and confirm the updated data from them to my spreadsheets, and adjust the projected future on the spreadsheets to account for any new changes.

It's not as daunting a task as it may sound. Since I have the entire year plan mapped out, it's simply a matter of inserting or deleting lines and adjusting some amounts here and there. But what you see is a running balance of your money projected over the course of the entire year, which gives you options and insight into how to plan your spending. Keeping that running balance on the pro-forma ledger alerts me to future problem spots, temporary cash shortage projections, that can be addressed and thwarted.

Or, conversely, it will reveal the extra cash periods, where I can sock away maybe a little more than planned. It is especially helpful when larger unforeseen amounts come in and go out, because I can project it's impact into the future and proactively adjust spending or savings to compensate.

Using this method consistently creates financial stability. Once that stability is achieved, I can focus on building a safe buffer. Once the safe buffer is achieved, I can then begin to start investing into more safe passive strategies, thus building wealth and true prosperity.

It doesn't matter which method you use, whether it be on a computer, paper, or dry beans in a can, so long as you do it, and do it consistently. Later I'll provide some more specific tips on what works for me.

But it all begins and ends with your mindset.

The Biggest Danger In Slipping On Your Commitment

I cannot state it enough. During those times when you are living in relative prosperity, making sure you're paying all your bills, all of them, on time, and earning a comfortable wage where you can afford to save money and begin to enjoy the finer things are the times where you are most at risk for sloughing on your commitment.

We fall into that false notion that happy days are here again, all of our financial woes are behind us, we believe the storm is over. So, we figure that things are going well now, we don't need to be so diligent with tracking our finances. We think we're in good shape now and don't have to worry about falling down anymore.

Wrong. Wrong, wrong, wrong, wrong, and wrong.

It is when you take your eyes off the ball that the pitcher serves up the wild pitch that dings you right in your mug (how's that for a 1940s idiom?). You find yourself, like many others, and with me perhaps the biggest offender of all, taking more and more liberties with your discretionary money. You've got some spare cash, so if you want something you get it. But what impact will that acquisition have on your financial profile six months or a year down the road?

This is precisely why it's important to stick with it. I use that dynamic combination ledger of what has financially happened and concise detailed budget of what I'll be bringing in and spending, projected over the course of the year. It will update and calculate my finances with every line addition in the daily maintenance, whether coming in or going out, and keeps a running balance of cash in the bank accounts and investments projected through the end of the year. It performs an immediate what-if analysis and allows me to see the impact of any added update item on the lean and prosperous weeks throughout the year.

I set a bottom limit of where I want to be with my working

checking accounts, which automatically generates a warning to me if any of the projected entries fall below that threshold.

This gives me an opportunity to adjust my spending or to ramp up earnings through side jobs or by selling assets (stuff) I don't need anymore, and overall to be more cognizant of my spending habits.

If I don't keep up with it how will I be able to discern the ebb times from the flow times? The beauty of it is that I can tell instantly more or less my financial profile in the near future, and avoid the pitfalls before I stumble into them. It lets me know when I can save more and when I will need to just stick to the minimums. Or if I need to further economize on non-essentials, at least for a while.

Successful businesses do it all the time. It's called financial forecasting.

By consistently monitoring it, or "minding the store" as I usually refer to it, there are much fewer surprises, and overall a more happy existence, you'll find.

A Few Early Tips

Before we get knee-deep in specifics, here's an early tip: I rarely deal in cash anymore, and only very occasionally use a credit card. Most of my purchases are made through my bank debit card, so I automatically have a record of my financial dealings. I keep a small cash reserve on hand and account for it on my spreadsheets as a blanket personal spending allowance. In business it's referred to as petty cash, but there's nothing petty about it. If we're not careful with it, it's frequently our downfall.

Some financial advisers say not to use your debit card for

anything; opt instead to use a credit card for most purchases and payments, for three main reasons: you automatically get fraud protection, you can collect credit usage points for cash-back programs, and your direct checking account is less exposed to being hacked.

In my case, I disagree with that warning. Since I check my bank account electronically several times per day, it's easy to track when pending charges hit your account. If one shows up, and it has in the past, I immediately flag it with my bank before the charge is posted and finalized, they'll kill the card and issue me a new one. In every instance I didn't incur the charges...because I was watching. I was minding the till. I monitor my account at least once a day, not allowing potentially fraudulent charges to get past the "pending" status. As for the credit card cash-back programs, I view that as an enticement to go running to your credit cards, causing the temptation for us to charge more than we can pay off. So I avoid it altogether.

If you choose to go the route of using credit cards for your purchases, that's fine, provided you resolve to pay off your charges every month, so that you don't carry credit card balances. More will be explained on that soon.

2 - Pay Yourself First

This is perhaps the second most important lesson to learn beyond the need to be consistently and personally engaged in effectively managing your finances. The age-old excuse that one cannot afford to save is a poor one, both figuratively and literally.

There's no way around it: the only way you save money is by saving it. Period. There are many ways of earning it, and many ways of spending it, but there is only one way to save it.

Most people would be amazed at what they spend on small items that they really don't need and wouldn't pay for if they didn't have the too-available cash in their pockets. Impulse buying is almost unavoidable; and it should not be avoided, but we have to be realistic about it. It's too easy for the money to slip from the pocket into the hand, from the hand to the cashier, and from the cashier to someone else's cash drawer. If not guarded, our pockets can soon be empty, and the cash register full.

Balance What's Coming In And Going Out

Naturally, if your regular bills exceed your income, severe

adjustments to your financial structure are in order. Make more money, spend less money, or a combination of both, until you at least reach equilibrium. You may need to go out and find extra work. If the disparity between what's coming in and what's going out is too great, you will then have to make some major lifestyle alterations in your big-ticket lifestyle.

The larger items, including savings, living accommodations, transportation costs, utilities, debt service, insurances, and food are indeed necessities, essentials. Note the first item in that list: Savings. View your savings as the most important regular bill that you need to pay to yourself. It is properly itemized as number one on the list. Pay yourself first. It's really that simple.

Remember this. Never, ever skip a payment to yourself. Make it your number one priority, condition yourself to the understanding that it's your most important bill. Over a short period of time in practice you'll come to see why. You've begun building a financial buffer that will thwart most future minor setbacks.

So How Much Do I Pay Myself?

Since you're in charge of setting your regular savings amount, how much should you plan on setting aside? It is suggested that you start light, say, five to ten percent of your take-home pay. Once you get in the habit of saving and enjoy the excitement of seeing your bank account steadily begin to grow over a relatively short period of time, you may want to slowly increase the percentage as a personal challenge to your frugality. But when starting out you should not set less than five percent, if you can. If you can't you'll need to make some behavioral adjustments.

Many of your regular bills are fixed amounts. Others, such as gasoline and utility bills, and revolving credit card bills, are determined by the amount of your usage. They are necessary but variable. Food is another variable necessity, and a big one that will be addressed separately.

When you're doing your initial planning, it's better to overestimate your variable expenditures; it's another way of tricking yourself into fewer surprises and ultimately saving more money. By doing so you're building into your plan a datapoint where you can economize in your projections down the road.

For example, after doing your regular updates you see that four months from now your budgeted balance is expected to dip below your personally set minimums. So you have a little play in your variable budgeted items you'll be able to cut back on temporarily. Particularly in the grocery store. You may not be able to afford those steaks as a regular staple for a few weeks. Switch to chicken or ground beef for those tight periods. Or even go vegetarian for a while, it'll probably help more than hurt anyway.

Drastic Measures

If you're financially bogged down after adding your essential expenses, as stated before, some major financial structural changes are required. Regarding economizing on your big-ticket essentials, brutal self-honesty is in order. You may have to make some compromises that you would rather not, but need to do nonetheless to ensure the chances of obtaining a prosperous future.

You may be living in more of a house than you really need. If you're a homeowner, maybe consider moving to a less costly alternative. Many people have homes much larger than they really need, only for the sake of appearances and status. Own your home, don't let your home own you.

On the other hand, if you're renting, make getting into home ownership primary in setting the priority of your longer-term goals. Doing so can be an excellent path to your eventual prosperity. When you rent, the only thing you get out of it when you move is: Out.

Ownership builds equity. There's a whole chapter in this book about living in your savings account, your paid-off home.

You may need to consider downsizing your vehicle. If you have a big gas-guzzling status symbol of a vehicle, do some research and find a vehicle that is more fuel efficient with high ratings and excellent service record. I know of someone who had a high-end Mercedes, and it looks really nice when driving through the neighborhood, but it costs $2,000 to replace a tail light.

Your status in keeping up with the Joneses is entirely your call, or I believe "flexing" is the current vernacular, but you have to be able to afford it. Bear in mind, it's not a contest.

More Economizing Tips

Other ways of economizing, and less dramatic ones in your lifestyle perspective, are to be more conscious of your energy usage by turning out lights and bumping your air-conditioning and heating up or down a degree or two, respectively. Wait until utility costs go down in the late evening hours of the day to run dishwashers or laundry equipment, when the rates are lower.

Check the temperature on your water heater. In my former home my water heater was originally set at 140 degrees, I lowered it to 120 degrees. It literally cut my electric bill in half, and I never suffered any cold showers. It seems I was just paying for the energy to keep the water scalding while it was sitting in the tank unused. Plus, there were less second degree burns.

If you smoke, quit. For a two-pack a day smoker, put that extra $6,000 per year into your mortgage, savings, or revolving credit bills.

Buy as little as you can manage on credit; credit usage is always some very expensive money. Much more on that later.

Avoid buying name brand items for many of the small items that you won't be frequently using. Focus on quality, intended frequency of use, and replacement costs as mitigating factors when contemplating the purchase of these items. Make sure you're not spending extra needlessly just for the brand name. For example, I occasionally need power tools for small home improvement projects. It doesn't benefit me to invest $300 in an electric drill, because I'm not in the construction industry and don't need to rely on such a costly tool on a daily basis. I will only use it occasionally around the house. A $25 drill will suffice.

Avoid impulse purchases as much as you can, and make as many of your purchases as possible considered and planned ones.

Bag It

The old saying goes that we don't live by bread alone is

partly true, but we do live by food. Of the necessary variable essential items, food is frequently our major source of over-spending, be it in the grocery store, the convenience store or the restaurant. With those you're not paying for nutrition, you're paying extra for convenience.

It's part of the programming in our service-oriented society these days. We're all running around serving each other, and paying dearly for the service, so that we can run around and serve each other.

Bagging a lunch or dinner is vastly superior, both in nutritional quality and wallet impact. The time we spend on serving others can be saved by serving ourselves.

Another problem in our consumer-based society is unnecessary consumption. The USA has the highest percentage of morbid obesity globally. We're conditioned for gluttony, and have learned the "live to eat" consumption culture rather than the "eat to live" mindset. Laden all of that fast food with mountains of refined sugar and you end up supporting not only the fast-food industry, but also the healthcare industry and big pharma as well.

Simple self-denial is more sensible if you can't pack a lunch. There's nothing wrong with waiting until you get home to eat a healthy and wholesome meal. Sadly, like personal financial responsibility, good nutrition has also fallen by the wayside in our life curricula. So has delayed gratification.

Don't Buy Food Just To Rot

It might take a little extra time to plan your meals and shopping ahead of time, but it is well worth it in the long run as an ongoing investment in your future. My grocery bills used to run $500-$800 per month, and I live alone. One day I had an epiphany that my refrigerator was being used as a long-term storage unit for rotting food. There were so many items I bought at the grocery store that spoiled before I even got to unpack them, let alone cook them. This was in part because I shopped when I was hungry, or because I impulsively just grabbed whatever suited my fancy at the moment. It's okay to pick up a few extra things that may not have made it to your shopping list, but look for deals on things, and on those that have a longer shelf life.

I now have a dry erase board on the wall in my kitchen, where I keep a running shopping list. I only put items on it that I know I'll be needing, when I notice I'm out or will be soon. I don't really deviate too much from that list. When I need to go grocery shopping, I simply snap a photo of the board on my cell phone.

For the most part I get what I need, I eat what I get, and I no longer buy too many short-shelf-life perishables. This has cut my grocery bill in more than half.

Sharpen Your Culinary Skills

Another helpful thing in the kitchen is to learn how to make meals from scratch. I love corn tortillas, store-bought prepared ones are fairly nominal in cost to begin with. Instead of buying the premade tortillas, I buy raw masa flour and now I make my own. Three ingredients: masa flour, water and a little salt. Many days I would eat just the fresh homemade tortillas, sometimes sandwiched with a little cheese as a rudimentary quesadilla, sometimes with thinly sliced avocado, sometimes with just a little butter melted on them. Occasionally with leftover chicken. Fresher, cheaper, healthier, and way more flavorful than store bought.

If you have leftovers, eat them before they spoil. Don't just stick them in the fridge and wait for them to turn into penicillin. Some meals last me three days, if I make something bountiful. Or, as is frequently the case, if there's not enough left over for a full meal I'll augment them with a newly added side-dish or main course. I used to joke that I ate leftovers every night, and can't even remember what the original meal was. It also helps sharpen your creative culinary skills.

Since I live alone, I've joined several groups that focus on cooking for one. I've learned many delicious, easily prepared nutritious dishes that create very little waste. If I do make too much, I'll freeze individual servings of what is left.

Save Dining Out For Special Occasions Only

Furthermore, in the past, while I was spending that ridiculous amount on groceries that would go uneaten, I was constantly on the go and found it was more convenient for me to dine out. Almost all the time. Not cheaper, but definitely more convenient. I was spending at least an additional $800 per month on dining out, and most of it was crap food anyway. I may eat out once a month these days, if that, and shy away from junk and extravagant food items. I will pack a lunch if I need to be out of the home, or just wait until I get home to eat. Again, it's cheaper and a whole lot healthier. My friends at the McRestaurant and convenience stores now miss me.

Remember, every step up from homemade results in higher preparation, packaging, and service costs. If you aren't already, get used to having those leftovers. What is convenient most of the time is also unnecessarily expensive. And definitely not as healthy in the long run.

Buy the giant family packs of meats and rather than just throwing the whole package in the freezer, break it down into meal-sized portions transferred into sealable freezer bags. You can get cost savings from the grocery store bulk packages, and repackaging them yourself will save you money over paying for the extra grocery store packaging.

There are numerous YouTube videos out there where people challenge themselves to extreme culinary frugality. Anyone who's made spaghetti from Ramen noodles and tomato soup in order to get by knows this. It's true that you can, if you're careful, feed a small family on $10 to $15 per week. But this is sustenance only, and at best only moderately healthy, at its best. To balance that, there are also many more how-to videos available showing you ways to make inexpensive raw ingredients into delicious healthy meals.

3 - Even More Economizing Tips

What Do We Want vs. What Do We Need?

After these essentials are satisfied what you have left is your regular discretionary spending, the little regular extra items and social goodies that make our lives enjoyable. The larger cable channel packages, recurring online service subscriptions, the taking unnecessary road trips, sticking a little too much cash in your pocket for convenience store coffees and snacks all have a cumulative effect on your financial profile, much more than most of us realize.

Again, resisting the keeping up with the Joneses trap, do you really need every cable TV channel under the sun? Does television consume a large part of your typical day? We've been subconsciously conditioned to believe that these are things that we need; that our life is not complete without them. We can sit dormant consuming copious bowls of imitation cheese flavored crunchy air balls while living our lives vicariously through a 55" inch flat screen. More consumer conditioning.

Most cable companies are structured with channel lineups in specific plans with channels that you cannot get a la carte. So to watch it you have to buy a package or an add-on. A possible cost saving idea is to make a list of what channels are absolute requirements for you and look for alternative ways of obtaining them. All a cable company is an aggregator of television channels. You can go and build your own channel lineup. Ask yourself, do they constitute an actual need?

I seldom watch TV, and I would cancel cable TV altogether, but in order to have internet service from my provider I have to take at least the minimum channel package. If I want to watch TV I can get plenty of free movies from a streaming TV device. There are many available out there. They are devices you own, and if you stay away from the paid services and stick with only free ones (there are plenty of them out there, so many that I would challenge you to find enough time to watch all of them...but make sure you keep up with your financial tracking in the process).

The Life Of Your Car

Your vehicle affords you many opportunities to save as well, without needing to downsize your existing one. Rather than just repeatedly dashing out to the store for something numerous times because you've run out of whatever it is, is a waste of fuel, and more; it is much better to "bunch" your trips. That is, plan every outing intentionally, go out once and knock as many out at one time as possible. You'll save on mileage, gas, money, and the life of your car.

This is another good reason to keep lists of what you need. I work mostly from home, and I might make a trip with stops at the post office, bank, hardware store, grocery store, pet store, and pharmacy in a single trip one day, and not need to venture out for several days afterwards. In addition to saving the gas from needless multiple forays into the wilderness, I'm also saving on the life of my vehicle. This is something that many folks caught up in the hustle and bustle of life overlook. Similar to heartbeats in a human, your vehicle has a finite number of miles it's going to be able to run before croaking. You take care of your health because you want to live longer and happier, and in addition to routine maintenance, so should you take care of your vehicle by extending the length of time it will be around to serve you.

Try to reduce the number of individual trips you take in order to increase the chances of achieving that; plus, an added bonus is you'll be saving on the frequency of maintenance and repair issues.

If you do work outside of the home, you'll need to be even more diligent in economizing on your non-commuting trips, because the commuting and work travel expenses also tick away your vehicle's lifespan.

As Americans, we've become so spoiled in our thinking that we need to have one, two, or more cars. Some people only have one, but get a new car that they finance every couple of years, which, while nice to have, is not really necessary. They trade in their cars, while still carrying a balance on the old car, and refinance their way into the new car. I've yet to see a car payment go down with every successive trade-in purchase. More typically people find themselves "upside down" in their vehicles; that is to say, they owe more than the asset is worth.

Pay your car off as early as possible. Not having a car payment is an automatic savings of several hundred dollars per month. But you say, "Yeah, but the older the car gets the more problems it starts to have."

Again, I say "Hogwash."

That's an excuse to maintain luxury and status, which are both terrific. But you have to be able to afford those luxuries.

Miserly or Frugal?

There are myriad ways to economize on your spending. Remember, it's not being miserly, it's being frugal. There's a huge difference. You can and should allow yourself life's little pleasantries here and there. The key to saving is being intentional about your spending and saving habits, rather than haphazard.

4 - The "Coffee Can" Saving Method

Putting ourselves on a modest cash allowance is another small way to trick ourselves into saving more money, if we primarily use our banking for most of our financial dealings. It simplifies our ledger-keeping process.

I call it the "Coffee Can Method," a holdover from the all-cash days of yesterday. This was a time when a little bit was set aside by mom or dad, whoever might've managed the family's finances, from each paycheck for family vacations, emergency funds, side-savings, etc. We give ourselves a cash allowance that we can spend on personal discretionary things, the total of which we account for in our formal budget tracking.

This way we don't need to track our individual cash dealings, and will still have the money accounted for in our ledgers. You can track every penny that's spent if you wish, but unless you're doing it to collect a specific dataset in order to put a really fine point on your precise spending habits, that data collection is not worth much and is very time consuming.

Keep the petty cash petty.

Drawing The Line

When it's all spent, it's crucial to keep in mind that's all until the next pay period. Knowing then that we have to be more selective with our discretionary spending might mean that we have a little left over when the next pay period comes around. The trick is to only replenish only what you've spent from your allowance from the period before.

For example, if I give myself an allowance of $150 for two weeks and I spend $110 of it over the period I'll have $40 left over at the next pay cycle. It'll only take $110 to bring me back to the $150 allotment for the next cycle. That extra $40 that I don't take in cash can then be squirreled away in my interest-bearing savings account.

Just because it is allotted to you does not mean you are required to spend it all. It's not a federal budget item, in that if you don't spend it in one fiscal period, you cannot justify asking for more in the next.

Every dime you don't spend is a dime you're saving. Some weeks I don't do any discretionary cash spending at all, so I get a free pass on savings.

5 – Easy Credit Ain't All That Easy

I recently watched a well-meaning but not particularly articulate YouTube video trying to explain the difference between simple and compound interest. All was good while explaining revolving credit but the presenter got tripped up when trying to explain the concept of loan amortization. They tried wading too deeply into the complex formulae that are used.

Indeed it can be a complicated concept to understand but the bottom line for both simple interest and amortized loans is that using money on credit can get pretty darned expensive. These days legitimate lenders are well regulated in what they can charge you for the use of their money, but the rates can range from slightly above the prime rate all the way up to nearly the usury levels of years past. And illegitimate lenders are much, much worse, if you value your kneecaps.

As mentioned, loan amortization can be a difficult concept to grasp at first but it becomes a quite simple concept if you take a little time to understand it. Surprisingly many people don't understand it simply because there's too much math involved, but it has a dramatic impact on the cost of the money you borrow. If you don't focus on the math, the method of how they arrive at the figures they do and just accept the formulae as the way of the world, the overall concept is easier.

You take a loan for a certain length of time at a certain percentage annual interest rate. A complicated formula is applied by the lender that will calculate the total amount you will have to pay for the original loan amount plus accumulated compounded annual interest over the length of the loan. That amount is divided by the number of total payments in the loan to give you your fixed monthly payments. You have at least two items that are included in your monthly payment, principal and interest. Mortgages also add taxes and property insurance into your monthly payment, and these amounts are put into escrow by the lender to cover those costs. Escrow is a holding account used as a fiduciary responsibility to hold someone else's money for a special purpose.

The monthly interest charged is based upon the current balance on the loan. The most important thing to remember with amortization is that the interest gets paid first out of that complicated formula that the lender used to calculate your payment. The balance you owe on the loan is then reduced by the difference between your fixed payment and the interest paid that month. For your first payment since you are paying mostly interest, very little is taken off of the balance due. Your second payment is also mostly interest, but ever so slightly less, because it's based upon how much you've paid down your loan so far (not much). For your final payment mostly the principal balance is reduced with very little charge in interest. You are charged interest monthly on the remaining balance, but the payment remains the same. The repayment is not linear, either, so you're actually not paying equal amounts of principal and interest until you're at about the two-thirds or even longer point through the term of the loan, depending upon the specific interest rate you're being charged.

This is why loan officers are happy to urge you to refinance your home after a few years. Toward the end of your loan they're making very little off of the debt in interest. It behooves them to dig in like a tick early.

Credit Card Trap

The biggest offenders in legal usury, though, are in credit cards and other revolving charge accounts, including home equity loans. People who use this open-ended form of credit are given a maximum amount the creditor is willing to risk on them, gleaned from their credit report numbers, and charge a relatively high interest rate based on the balance outstanding.

The old adage states that to obtain financing means that you first have to prove that you don't need it. If you can prove that you might get a more favorable interest rate; but if you don't, you'll pay up to the highest rate allowed by law to cover the lender's risk.

Your minimum payment every month will change as you exercise the use of that credit. It's an open-ended proposition with no termination in sight unless the borrower (you) takes steps to clear out the debt. With credit cards you are charged monthly on your outstanding balance, at an annual interest rate that can run in the 20% to 30% range, or possibly more, up to the legal maximum depending upon where you live. If you pay only the minimum amount due each month it will take you decades to pay it off. The majority of people sadly only pay the minimum amount every month.

It's like making a new mortgage that you grant anew every month with each payment you make being the first mostly-interest payment on that loan. The lenders love it.

For example if you have a credit card account with a $10,000 limit at 24% simple interest and essentially keep using it to it's max, your balance due will remain at the maximum, which means you cannot use it anymore, or at least very little, and the interest you're paying monthly alone is around $200 per month or more for that privilege. Your balance might decrease a little, but the majority of the payment goes to interest. They calculate your minimum payment to be ever so slightly above the interest due, so that it creates the illusion that you're getting yourself out of debt.

As a case in point, at one time in the past I had two credit cards, one with a $12,000 credit limit and one with a $3,600 limit. I ran each of them up to about 80% of their maximum, and was carrying a total of about $12,000 worth of debt between the two. This is also considered excessive by the credit reporting agencies and negatively impacts your credit profile. And your credit rating is what determines the percentage your lender will charge you for renting their money. Starting to see the cycle yet?

I was paying more than the minimum amount they said was due in an effort to pay down my debt. For both cards together I was told by the credit card companies that the total of the minimum payments was about $300, basically interest-only. But in an effort to pay down the debt I was adding at least an extra $100 most months, paying out a minimum of $400. Of the $400 I was paying, around $300 of it went to debt service interest and the extra $100 or so was taken off of the balance owed.

It's calculated so that, absent any positive action on your part, you will remain in debt servitude nearly forever. Put simply, it's a debt slavery trap. You will be controlled by maintaining a debt at or near the maximum risk, and the declining numbers on your credit report will continue to render you into a higher-percentage category. Sometimes in perpetuity. Sadly, we've become a nation of debtors.

I finally got out of it by taking a 5 year personal consolidation loan for $15,000 to pay off the outstanding credit card balances and the small remaining mortgage balance on my home. Nine years ago I needed to borrow a relatively small amount to round out the purchase of my home, $20,000 amortized over 15 years. My mortgage payment was around $260 per month, a nominal amount, but I also paid extra on the note every month to get to an earlier payoff. My payoff was about $3,500, so I included that in the consolidation loan and paid off my 15 year mortgage in just under 10 years.

The end result, the before and after picture:

- Before - Paying out $700-$800 per month for two credit cards with very slowly decreasing balances and a low home mortgage payment

- After - Consolidation loan payments for 5 years at $325 per month, but I paid an extra $175 per month on the loan, totalling $500 per month, which reduced the balance monthly and the loan's term to 3 years instead of 5, thereby saving more than $2,000 in the consolidation loan interest over the life of that consolidation loan. The penalty I paid in taking the loan was a front-loaded loan origination fee, but in the long run was worth it.

Bear in mind the interest rate for the consolidation loan was only slightly more than my mortgage interest rate, but I viewed it this way: My home mortgage payment would have been roughly the same for the next three years as the basic loan consolidation payment, so the $175 extra per month is what I was actually paying for the debt service from the credit cards. In my view $175 to the amortized consolidation loan lender is less than $350 per month in the combined interest I would have otherwise been paying. Plus that'd be one less check I'd have to write every month. Except for my vehicle payment I'm now living debt-free. And my credit rating has improved dramatically.

6 - Live In Your Savings Account

Conventional financial wisdom says you should leverage your equity in your investments. It's an alluring thought, but as we have seen, people don't always figure on the cost of money. You're sucked in by the promise of refinancing, or second- and third- mortgages on property, so you can "make your equity work for you." This is a sham come-on designed to keep you in debt forever. Beware the money changers.

What Is A Mortgage?

If you're fortunate enough to call yourself a homeowner, chances are that you're on the hook for at least one mortgage. Few consider from where the term "mortgage" derives, its etymology.

Mortgage comes from two old French words, "mort," and "gage." "Mort" means dead, and "Gage" means pledge. Taken together it's literally a "dead pledge" that you're in fact granting, in other words, a promise until death. It was a way land barons of yesteryear could dupe the masses into thinking they owned their own real property, but it was effectively a rental for life. True, the ownership of the real property carried to the purchaser, but that ownership was subject to the terms of the mortgage. If you didn't pay it you would eventually become homeless and lose whatever equity you had amassed. Originally it was until they sold the property or died, in either case the land baron would just take a mortgage ("dead pledge") from the next occupant. And as an added bonus it relieved the land baron from tort liability. It was touted as an affordable way for a regular citizen to become a landowner, but it actually was a wolf in sheep's clothing.

In more recent history the terms have been standardized to lengths of a determinate time, typically 15- or 30- years. As stated earlier, for every payment you make, the interest on the loan comes first, based upon your loan balance. For the first years of your mortgage, most of your payments cover the interest, with a very small amount deducted from the principal balance.

Over the life of a 30-year mortgage on a home you've bought for $250,000 at 4% annual interest, you'll be paying out a total of around $430,000 at nearly $1,200 per month excluding taxes and insurance. Many people only live in a house for a few years, then trade up, which is great for the lenders, because they get to start all over with a front-end loaded interest income source on a new mortgage.

Those they can't coerce into moving to other digs are then inundated with offers to leverage their equity in their homes by enticing them to either refinance or take out second and third loans on the property.

Who Owns Whom?

Too many folks think they own their homes, when it's actually the other way around: their homes own them. I have a family member who has a lovely home. He has made it a beautiful gathering place for the entire family. He and his wife both have professional jobs, and they're getting to the age where they want to retire but cannot because of the blistering mortgage they're strapped with. What good is a half-million dollar or more home if you're too busy paying for it to enjoy it? I feel badly for them. They are owned by their home; or rather, by the financial obligations on their home.

For my last three homes, I always paid down more than the monthly payment to reduce the principal balance as much as possible so I wouldn't be hit with so much interest over the life of the loan. And the extra paid down on the mortgage reduced the overall term of the loan, and increased my equity position. Every extra bit you pay on a mortgage reduces the calculated interest/principal ratio. In one extreme case, we were able to pay off a 30-year mortgage in 7-½ years, by exercising good financial practices and paying at least double for every monthly payment. This required us denying ourselves a lot of extra luxuries, but it paid off in the long run.

In a sense, the satisfaction you get from making that last payment on a mortgage is tremendous, and it is a major payment thereafter that just simply goes away. Sure, you still need to carry homeowner's insurance and pay your property taxes, but that's usually a drop in the bucket compared to a mortgage loan/interest payment. After that act of self denial where you pay off your home loan early, you can tuck away what you had been paying into savings. Therefore it can be rightly said that you are living in your savings account. If anything catastrophic were to occur in the future, you'd still have an option of going to the money-changers again as a last resort.

The Game Isn't Over For Renters

If you are renting and not a homeowner, your first priority should be to work towards getting yourself into a position of home ownership as quickly as possible. For most, it will be a fairly long-term goal, but should be viewed as a necessary one. Down payments can be as little as 5% for FHA-backed mortgage loans, or 0% if you have had prior military service through the VA. Bear in mind that FHA loans are insured, where VA loans are guaranteed.

When the time is right, find a home that is what you can modestly afford to purchase and pay for, while still proactively building your savings.

How can you tell when the time is right? When you've saved enough cash to cover a down payment with enough left over to have a comfortable emergency fund is the safest time to get into home ownership. And just as important, a home where, if you factor it into a what-if scenario with your finances, you'll be able to still save money while making the payments. Again, you might scoff and say that it's impossible, it's too lofty a goal. But the truth is it is not impossible if you set your mind and resolve on it.

Resign yourself to the idea that you won't start out with your dream castle on the hill. But it will at least be something that you can call your own. Having home rehab skills is an added bonus, because with a little imagination and sweat equity, fixer-uppers at a decent price increases your options, and rapidly increases your overall equity in the home.

Stay away from those rent-to-own deals. They may seem to be great opportunities, and they might be, but more often they are basic land installment contracts, where if you ever fall behind in your payments you can legally be evicted. For example you may rent to own a dwelling with terms that last ten years. If, in the eleventh month of the ninth year you might miss the grace period on the payment by one day the actual homeowner of record, your landlord, technically can obtain a judgement and evict you. Since you've lived in the home for nearly ten years and treated it as your own, handling repairs and upgrades, you could be sorely disappointed. Any default on the note can be grounds for the owner, who still retains legal title to the home.

Real estate scams are a dime-a-dozen. Beware of them, and the best way to circumvent them is to go the traditional route by dealing with realtors, home inspectors, reputable title and escrow companies, and reputable financiers. And even then you will need to watch carefully. Quick/easy deals are fraught with potential dangers. In real estate especially, *caveat emptor*, let the buyer beware.

It may take you several years to achieve this, depending upon how long it takes you to save. All the more reason for you to be very serious about saving as much as you can and being meticulously scrupulous with your spending habits.

Remember, this is a life-long building process.

7 - Build A Buffer

All along I've stressed the need for you to save money, that you actually can afford to save it, but to do so you have to work on it. Your savings, often viewed as a Rainy Day Fund, gives you the ability to weather the occasional ups and downs that life serves up to us all from time to time. Not having a savings buffer when I was a younger full-time musician created much panic and stress, where one lost day of work would set us back weeks or months.

Conventional financial wisdom says that you would need to have enough savings tucked away to cover at least three to six months of living expenses if suddenly nothing was coming in. An even stronger ideal says twelve months. The first time I heard that I laughed. "No way," I said.

But, after disciplining myself to closely watch my finances, living smaller than my prior lifestyle could afford, slowing down, and having built enough savings to sustain me indicates to me that I have achieved the goal, it's incredibly stress-relieving. You sweat the small stuff a lot less when you have a buffer in place to absorb the downturns.

Not The End Game

The six months of living expenses should also be an interim goal, a marker to let you know you're doing it right. Hopefully by reaching that milestone you would have accumulated the skills required for you to make your newfound financial awareness skills into a lifelong habit rather than a chore.

This is especially to say that one should neither heavily nor frequently rely on dipping into their Rainy Day Fund savings, it must be carefully and judiciously meted out. A strategy to prevent the pillaging of your savings is to set an arbitrary amount that no matter what, you're not going to let the balance drop below XXX number of dollars, and reserve the right to increase that amount as you build your wealth. But never justify lowering that balance to accommodate something that you only want, rather than need, to have. That is a sure path to self-sabotage.

Use it only for what you absolutely need, or have calculated as a wise investment risk that will provide further financial gain and security. Be very conservative with those risks.

8 - Taking Charge

This is what it's all about: taking charge of your personal finances affords you many more options that living a week to week, paycheck to paycheck lifestyle would not. It's not that money supersedes anything else in your life, but keeping it in its proper place allows a much simpler and more satisfying life, and ultimately can enhance your overall health and happiness. And that of your family.

It can only be done by focusing your intent and steadfastly applying hard work to get there; the unfortunate truth is that even then the fates will occasionally have a say in the matter.

Quantum Schmuantum - Throw Out Wishful Thinking

When I say focus your intent, it is not in some nouveau "quantum jumping" sense, the Einsteinian "spooky action at a distance" kind so popularly tossed about these days. The get-rich-quick gurus have lately adopted "quantum jumping" or "quantum leaping" as buzzword phrases by appropriating quantum physics into their platitudes. With only a minimum understanding of the real physics involved they will proffer it as a circumvention of actual physics. Quantum science is indeed a real thing, but it's a reboot of the regular physical laws on a subatomic level rather than on the level of our full-sized perceived physical lives. There is an element of truth to it, but the words "jumping" or "leaping" in these phrases remove it from validity.

These gurus who have sold you their schemes will tell you that you only need to focus your intent to get what you want. They build an out for themselves if it doesn't work by suggesting that if it doesn't, you're not doing it right. They'll suggest that you're not focusing your intention properly. The terms "quantum jumping" or "quantum leaping" are oxymorons in themselves. Quantum physics is a set of rules; it is static. The action words added to the end of the phrases are the devil in the details. They imply action, as in all you have to do is wish, and wish fervently, and it will become so. This is flawed thinking. Merely wishing ain't going to make it so.

The truth of the matter is the duality of nature requires two things for animation to occur, to bring something into creation: a spark and a container. More appropriately an idea and an action. An idea, a sentence, at minimum is a noun and verb. Wishing is an action, sure, but it's an action that requires no actual doing.

The get-rich-quickers will only tell you the spark of inspiration, the will, the intent part as a magical means to have anything you desire. The implication is that you can elevate your station in life by simply wishing for it. While wishing doesn't make it so, it is a start. What they don't tell you is that you must take a positive action for the actual creation to be completed.

The so-called financial wizards use the term "quantum jumping" to replace what is more correctly described as willpower. Oxford defines willpower as "control exerted to do something or restrain impulses." Noun and active verb are in that definition.

The spark and the container must both be present for creation to occur. The dream, notion, inspiration, or idea is the spark. Taking the proper steps, hard work, and diligence to achieve is the container. Without either there's nothing but potential.

When Leveraging Can Be Beneficial

Leveraging is using your equity as security to borrow, hopefully where the risk-to-benefit ratio is favorable. You adopt something akin to the strategy of the robber-baron, albeit much less cut-throat.

Where the question of leveraging your financial profile is concerned, it can indeed be a worthwhile proposition, but it should never be a risk that you cannot afford. You should only risk actual equity, and only do so if you're prepared to absorb it if things start going south.

For a very general rough example, two people might hear of a "sure thing" bet in an upcoming horse race. Both want to bet $1,000 on the race in the hopes of attaining a huge payout. But one has socked away enough mad-money to be able to cover the bet without it having any significant impact on his life. The other man goes to a high interest strip-store loan company and borrows the $1,000 at a ridiculously high short term interest rate. Both place their bets on the "sure thing."

But during the race the horse fails to cooperate.

Both men have leveraged something as a risk for a large return, one based upon an affordable tangible and one based upon a costly promise. One man has lost a bit of discretionary funds, but the other has set himself back financially months or years trying to recover.

Granted, the previous example is not strictly leveraging, and more to the point on the contrast between acceptable and unacceptable risk, but the general concepts of leveraging are there. Leverage is a form of risk where you are gambling something you have of value to achieve a more favorable outcome, to increase your value over time.

In both cases above the Win Tickets were the risk point, an unknown potential of increased wealth. In the former case the bettor leveraged his existing assets, his spare spending money cash, to place his wager. He used a tangible asset in his risk. In the latter case the bettor leveraged a promise and not a tangible asset. Therefore he increased his risk exponentially. Had the horse actually won the race, he would've kept his promise in repaying the note and enjoyed the financial increase that was left over. Instead, he placed himself in a deeper financial hole.

The moral of the story: In any risky new venture, whether it be at the betting window or in, say, real estate dealings or a new business startup, the proper use of leveraging is to secure the venture with assets that you can actually absorb if the risk takes a downturn.

Leveraging can be a powerful tool that you can use to work for you, especially in the purchase of a new home, but you must be very judicious with its use. There are a great deal of people out there who show enormous wealth on paper, but are leveraged to the hilt. They're only wealthy on paper.

It is a provocative way of having the false image of financial success. Be wary of falling into that trap. A good rule of thumb if you decide to go the leveraging route is to be realistic about what your actual balance sheet looks like, never take it into the red if there is a pathway to avoid it, and don't even think about beginning to use it until you've built yourself a comfortable financial buffer.

Avoid the appearance of prosperity, and work towards actual prosperity. Going for the appearance of being prosperous is a trap. I know many farmers who you wouldn't know from appearances how wealthy they actually are, but they are some of the most well off people I've ever met. Their balance sheet is as far away from seeing any red ink as you can imagine, and they have the means to pay cash for any purchase they care to make. But you'll still see them in old coveralls mucking livestock stalls. Looks can be deceiving.

9 - Invest and Diversify

You might tend to think that most of my focus here has been on the premise that "cash is king." That I eschew ever using leverage as a tool for building prosperity. This is emphatically not true. Cash is your safety net if you have it. And you should have it. Once you've saved enough of it you can then begin to use the amounts over and above your buffer savings to start passively generating income for you. But you have to protect it by applying diligent risk management.

A savings nest egg is good to have, but you should never put all of those eggs in one basket. The father of a dear lifelong friend worked very hard for his entire life, provided for his large family during his working years, was responsible and diligent with his earnings, and socked it all away in a savings account at the local savings and loan. One day, the owner of the savings and loan was toppled by a scandal which brought about a run on the institution, and forced the savings and loan to ultimately close its doors. Unfortunately my friend's father did not get in line in time to get his life savings out and lost it all.

Yes, it really happened. And can happen again.

Once you are successful in achieving a modest amount of savings you should start thinking about diversifying where you're putting your money. This will give you opportunities to start investing and start having that money to go to work for you.

Opening An Investment Account Is Easy

Much of society today runs on MHC (minimal human contact). This includes many online stock brokerage accounts. If you have any particular phobias about being perceived as stupid or vulnerable when dealing with a stockbroker, or feel like you just don't have enough investment assets to get the broker's full attention, there are fairly simple options for you.

There are reputable web-based stock broker portals out there where you can very simply establish a brokerage account with a few keystrokes from the comfort of your home. Stick with the larger outfits.

Since investment interest rates have been traditionally low in recent years, you may not be getting the best return on your regular savings account.

Steer away from day trading unless you become an expert at finances. This is a specialty niche in the financial markets world. Like horse racing, you cannot always rely on the "hot tips." To be a successful day-trader, as many are, you'll find that watching the ticker will consume much if not most of your day. Remember, you want your investments to provide passive income. Find these stocks, buy them and sit on them. I invested in QQQ stock (NASDAQ composites, because I correctly believed tech stocks were in their infancy) in 2003 and as of this writing my investment has increased by more than 1,300 percent.

Conservative investments into stocks and mutual funds,

especially in well-trod solid historically performing territory are usually the best. They may not provide the fastest growth, but there's a minimum of risk involved. Pick securities that have consistently performing growth or dividend numbers. With mutual funds, you can set your account to reinvest the dividends rather than cashing out whenever they're paid.

Also, invest in several types of brokerage accounts. I have three: a regular brokerage account, a traditional IRA and a Roth IRA. Most of my funds are conservative in nature and in my IRAs for retirement, and my brokerage account is for more risky speculation. I use the nominal amount in that account for occasional high potential growth stocks.

As in horse racing, there's no sure thing. Don't wager what you cannot afford to lose.

Diversify

Avoid leaning too heavily on one particular financial sector in your market dealings. Diversification is a risk management strategy that can mitigate all but the most dire of market downturns.

I like to stick with tech stocks for slightly riskier ventures, and protect that by investing in other sector-wide funds. If one company goes down in a particular sector, the rest will remain propped up and you'll be better off than having it all in one company. Remember the story of my friend's father with the savings and loan?

Balance the minimum risk with the maximum risk stocks in appropriate measures, that is, less in the riskier with a higher ultimate payout and be more vested in those traditional conservative steady performing stocks.

Another way to diversify, is as in the case of the defaulted savings and loan, to not put all of your nest eggs in the stock market. It's a good place to have your cash working passively for you, but you'll also want to have other means of saving.

Physical precious metals can be a good way to protect your financial portfolio. The raw metals, such as silver, gold, platinum and palladium, have a somewhat volatile but generally safe investment profile in the long haul. You just really need to buy low, and sell high, and be aware. If you're not numismatically inclined, an even better investment is to buy slabbed numismatic coins, collectors coins that have been professionally graded. They all go up over time in value.

Avoid, however, buying coins that are not professionally slabbed and graded, especially buying those at auction that might be touted as being uncirculated when they in fact are not sealed in a plastic slab and have not been professionally registered and graded. If you're not an expert numismatist, it's easy to be burned.

Likewise, purchasing fine art can be a highly profitable investment. But you have to have some savvy in that particular field, as well as have the storage space that is secure enough to hold it.

Deal With Stock Market Downturns

Those who are new at market investing will tend to panic when there's a significant downturn in their stocks. If you've properly mitigated your risk you can weather those storms, which do blow up from time to time, by holding fast. Even when every fiber of your being is telling you to sell short to cut your losses. It's a sucker bet. Hold the line, hold fast, resist panic selling. Tell yourself that you're in this for a long term payout. The market has, even through times of recession and depression, always returned and increased over time.

Only a few times with more speculative investments have I ever lost my entire investment in a particular stock. But then, I had diversified my portfolio enough and knew the stocks were risky to begin with and had only a minimal exposure in them, so the loss was more than offset by the gains I received from the remainder of my portfolio.

If a particular stock starts to dip, depending on the amount I have invested and the likelihood that the stock will return only after a modest dip, I might double down on them and purchase more of the stock, but never to a point of being oversaturated in them.

I'll dollar-cost-average my investment. These happenings are rare, and I've only done that a handful of times. But it has worked out more often than not that I've at least lost nothing and gotten free stocks out of it. Only once or twice did the stock completely tank and become worthless. I had a nominal investment anyway, only a figurative $2 win bet on it, but that's horse racing. The trick is to win some more than you lose some.

For example, say I buy 100 shares of a stock at $10 per share. I've got $1,000 invested in the company. If the stock, say, was to go down in a major sector downturn to $5 dollars a share, I might, especially if the forecasts indicate that it will recover, buy another hundred shares for $500. Then I'd own 200 shares that I had a total invested of $1,500, meaning I'd have to see the stock rise again to only $7.50 per share to get back to even. If it rebounded back to $10 per share, I could sell it all and profit $500.

But what I'd more likely do is sell 150 shares at the $10 per share price, recover my cash, and retain 50 shares as free stock. If that stock went up further, I'd still be staked, and if it went down I wouldn't have lost a dime.

When Do I Divest?

Typically I try to never divest my stocks. I have had financial need in the past to do a sell off, but still retained at least a nominal share in my best performers. And steadily added to my portfolio as a way of recovery afterwards.

If you are fortunate enough to invest in enough high dividend yielding stocks, rather than reinvesting the dividends, you can take money out of those. If you've socked away enough it can be a partial or complete source of your income. It would take a great deal of funds in your portfolio to achieve that, but it is actually being done. The key is to start early in life, be consistent with your contributions, and be lucky enough to pick many more winners than losers. But it is indeed possible

Bear in mind, though, that different account types have different tax implications. Some you'll be taxed at the capital gains rate, some as regular income, and some are tax free. I'm not a licensed financial advisor, so you should consult your accountant to explain the differences.

If the idea is to build this section of your portfolio so that you may supplement or completely rely on passive residual income to live, I would advise to never divest these accounts. The only exception to it is when you have a dire need for cash.

Finally, you should endeavor to periodically keep investing

in your funds, even after you retire. By then hopefully you will have been, through developing these habits, to be enculturated into the idea of regularly saving. So then that for whatever you regularly take out, you keep building your portfolio by turning a like percentage back. By turning your habitual savings plan back into those investments, you essentially take it out only to return a portion...it's another way to keep up with the habit and keep building your wealth.

A good general rule of thumb is to use your bank savings as a clearing house for your investment portfolio. In the same way you apportion your regular income into savings, living expenses, and discretionary funds, you likewise should apportion your savings account periodically into your other investments.

Diversifying your money is a great way to hedge your bets and keep most of your money safe. It's a conservative strategy for protecting yourself.

Cryptocurrency

Within the past decade the concept of digital money, cryptocurrency has been all the rage. Few people except the nerdiest really understand the depths of it, the technology that defines precisely what crypto is, but that doesn't really matter to most folks. Basically, it's an electronic representation of money.

It actually makes sense. Hard cash is used as a medium of exchange. And it's arbitrary on a global scale; it has almost no actual value except for the linen and cost of the ink. Look at fluctuations in trade currency rates over the planet. It has variable value.

Physical money only has a fiat value. That is, it's intrinsically worthless, except for the value that everyone agrees that it possesses. In recent years, much banking has been done through another form of digital currency: bank transfers. You may have direct deposit from your employer, you pay for purchases using your debit and hopefully not your credit cards, you pay your mortgage, car payments, utility bills, online purchases, etc., over the internet. It's just exchanging something of an agreed upon value. It's all virtual money. Properly secured bank transfers are essentially no different than cryptocurrency. With one difference.

It makes sense that someone would eventually come up with the idea of creating a private currency. A fixed number of arbitrarily valued virtual currency tokens to be used in trade, and can be traded in exchange for real dollars, or pounds, or Euro, or yen. The value of the cryptos has fluctuated wildly over time.

The first Bitcoin purchase in 2010 was by a Florida man who paid 10,000 Bitcoin to buy two pizzas. At that point in time, when it was new and not many people grasped the concept of virtual currency, the value of it was low. As of July 2021, those pizzas ended up costing $330 million.

Those fluctuations have begun to stabilize somewhat, but the fluctuations are still wide. Digital currency is likely here to stay. As long as there's an internet there will be digital currency. Many futurists predict that we are not far off from a completely cashless society.

Understanding that the fluctuations in the value can be severe, it makes sense to invest at least a small amount regularly into Bitcoin, or similar high performing cryptocurrency. The good thing about Bitcoin is that it's the first to hit the marketplace, is now becoming more and more accepted by vendors, and we are finally starting to see Bitcoin banks appear. It's indeed here to stay, but, like the stock market, their value is fluid, and therefore somewhat risky.

Trading in Bitcoin is a strategy, but I would caution against becoming a day trader. Like stock market day trading it can consume all of your time to keep up with it. If you choose to invest at least a small portion of your portfolio into cryptocurrency, use dollar-cost-averaging over a longer term, always applying the strategy of buying low and selling high. The market is so unpredictable, though, you must be careful.

Above all, unless this is your full-time job, and there are crypto day traders out there, for most people it makes sense to only visit it every few months or so. If the market is down, hold off on selling, and consider the risks of buying more. Conversely, if it is up, sell a portion. Every profit cycle increases your wealth. Set rigid rules for yourself for every time you periodically check on your crypto markets, as to whether to buy, hold, or sell. And if you sell, don't sell all, hedge your bet. Above all, never risk more than you're willing to lose.

10 - Go Rogue

The Covid-19 pandemic of 2020 brought many people into a position of financial uncertainty and panic, and sadly some to ruin. Most at risk were the millions who did not have a formalized savings plan and had no buffer to sustain them, and at worst, with no in-demand marketable skills, nor much in the way of skills for diversification.

Moreover, the employment landscape changed. Jobs and careers were lost throughout the shutdown process. Entire businesses, the majority of which were small cottage businesses, had to close their doors. Government stepped in to help through massive relief distribution and imposed a moratorium on evictions.

But when things began to open back up in mid-2021 and some available jobs again returned, not many have flocked back to them. A recent report indicated that more new small businesses have been started since June 2021 than in our nation's long history. This indicates a rebirth of the entrepreneurial spirit, and more.

The pandemic changed many aspects of our regular lives. It is conjectured that the shut-ins, because of job loss or reduction, have been squeezed into economizing in their lives. Of necessity they changed their spending habits, and post lockdown have found that they don't really need all of the stuff that they originally thought they did. This may have triggered the spontaneous implementation of many of the tidbits of advice offered in this book. If there is a silver lining to the life-changing pandemic lockdown, this is it.

But that could mean that people don't need as much cash and therefore feel that they don't need to earn as much. All well and good, but the continuing habits and attitudes of not being able to afford saving linger.

What can you do if you're coming up short and are still having difficulty making ends meet? Maybe you were able to work throughout the pandemic. If you held a clerical job you may have been fortunate enough to telecommute and work from home. Some of you had to endure pay cuts just to retain employed status.

You've learned to cut back on discretionary spending, yet you still have difficulty paying all of the bills, let alone build any savings. What are your options?

Let's go back to the basics. Again, there are two ways of economizing in your life: earn more and/or spend less. If you've reached your spend less limit, that leaves you with one option: earn more.

What Is Your Skillset?

There are things that you can do that not many people, and perhaps no one else, can.

In the past, in lean times, especially in my music days, I would take on temporary part-time work. I worked in a printing company hauling trash out to the dumpster (and was able to take home reams of paper that had not been correctly cut to size...high quality glossy printing press paper, too). For a time I worked in a dairy, processing WIC claims. And another time I conducted telephone interviews for data collection. Fortunately it was not telemarketing, and I was kind, friendly and congenial enough to get folks to answer some questionnaires over the phone, for which I was paid $2.50 for every three interviews that were completed. I could turn maybe 9 or 10 interviews in an hour. That's not much these days, but it was worth a lot more in the mid-70s. It wasn't much then, either, but at least it was something that just required me to talk to people, something I enjoy doing.

In more recent times I would go out and deliver food via one of the mass services (e.g., Uber Eats, DoorDash, GrubHub, Postmates, etc.). The compensation varied and was unpredictable from day to day, but I could generate $15 to $20 per hour doing that, and had the additional benefit of being able to have a completely flexible schedule. I could work whenever I wanted, for the most part, and got to meet a variety of new folks that I otherwise never would have.

The down side to that is where I was harboring no illusions about the fact that I was trading the life-mileage on my vehicle for income. This brought my net profit down significantly, but the gross amounts taken in were a short term solution. Plus I was able to deduct mileage, which favorably impacted my taxes.

I also entered the world of internet task jobbing. I registered with a number of research outlets, who, on occasion if I fit their survey demographic profile, would be offered small task jobs. They didn't pay much but required no more than me sitting on the web and answering a few questions. I might get paid $5 for a single task of reviewing web pages, which would take me 20-30 minutes, but it's money that I wouldn't otherwise be earning.

Every little bit helps. As Ben Franklin pointed out, "Mind the pennies and the dollars will take care of themselves."

I also keep my eyes open for opportunities which require a more specialized skill set. In my professional training I was qualified as an AV technology specialist, and occasionally got offers for contract work doing control system programming or system design. These jobs can be very lucrative, especially for longer term complex contracts.

I further use my CAD skills at doing technical drawings on a contract basis. In the past few years I entered a contract to provide as-built drawings for a security company at a fixed rate per drawing, and there were hundreds of drawings that needed to be done. Each one took less than an hour on average, so that was quite lucrative.

I currently provide music engineering, recording mixing and mastering services, and typically work on mastering two or three CD releases per year. I also offer expert podcast editing services. There are many bid job outlets on the web that have available contracts specific to your skills.

None of this is offered in any braggardly way. Rather, it is to illustrate that you may have talents that are exploitable that you never considered. Again, this is borne out by the recent surge in new small business startups.

So, what do you excel at? Is there anything you can do better than anyone else? Seek the work and it will find you.

Make A List, Keep Checking Twice (and More)

As has been stated, a method of bringing in more cash is to have as many irons in the fire as you have outlets available for your skills. None of them may pay much individually, but by putting them together, they begin to add up.

For every avenue you're seeking, every iron you have in that fire, you should keep a detailed list of what you've applied for, its payment amount and terms, and a guesstimate of how much time and effort it's going to take you to complete it. Stay up with that list, and transfer those that are "probables" and "definites" onto a work calendar. You can keep the calendar on your cell phone.

Keep the calendar and your master lists up to date to minimize the risks of becoming overextended to a point where you cannot deliver your contracts on time. The basic premise is that if you can't earn a lot doing one thing, do a lot of little things that will add up.

Again, it takes personal discipline. I cannot stress this enough. It's your only path to financial independence, barring hitting that one in a 100 million lotto ticket. Frankly, and not to be a Debby Downer about it, you're more likely to get struck by lightning while fending off a shark attack than hitting that big lotto jackpot.

Keep Your Promises

Just because any independent contract work you obtain may not pay much money is no excuse for offering less than your best professional attitude. Deliver on your promises to the best of your ability. Under promise and over deliver. It will get you asked back to the dance. It's that simple.

When You Get Paid

Neither should you skimp on your lists when you've completed a contract job, on any scale, from a $5 contract to a $50,000 one. Keep a record and be meticulous of your payments received and expenses incurred that are not reimbursed. It will come in very handy at tax time. If you have larger contract services work, make sure to set aside a portion as a tax withholding. I use a separate interest-bearing checking account to escrow enough to cover my tax burden at the end of the year. You may have penalties for not filing quarterly, but in my personal view the penalties outweigh the quarterly effort on collating and reporting. Call it a personal indulgence, the IRS doesn't mind imposing the penalty. But that's just me. You make the call.

The bottom line: as in your personal finances, track every dime that comes in and goes out, and do it religiously. It will save a mountain of time when tax time comes around, and perhaps save hundreds or thousands in accountant's fees.

11 - My Way Of Tracking Finances

It Works For Me!

Doing all of this on a PC is the easiest, least time-consuming, and most convenient way for me to track my finances, because it's easier to update spending and income by simply adding lines to a template structure and your bottom line is automatically recalculated for you, on a continuously updated basis. It's not the only way of doing it, but it certainly is the least time-consuming. I'm offering this as a possible alternative for you, and no matter which method you'll end up using, you can get an idea of what specific details to be aware of in keeping accurate, and with the most rudimentary

What I use is essentially a combination of a ledger/budget/forecasting/snapshot tool all in one. I have worked with spreadsheets for years, but by no means am an advanced spreadsheet programmer. The sheets only contain simple replication, requiring no more than simple addition and subtraction formulae, copied many times over.

There are programs that will do much of this work for you, many of them online and in the cloud. They're nice but there are a couple of downsides to them:

- They are usually subscription services that cost money that you don't need to spend if you simply do it yourself. The wood smells sweeter when burning when you've chopped and stacked it yourself, rather than from paying someone to dump it off of a pickup truck into your yard.

- They can take an inordinately long time to get set up and can be very confusing to operate, because they're generic and not tailored to your special circumstances. With your own method that you develop you'll understand every in and out of your method. Just make sure to be thorough. With these subscription services, your credit cards and banking will be automatically updated, which tends to make us start taking our money for granted. And that's somewhat antithetical to the entire exercise of learning to watch your money to begin with. It tends to deprive you of the pleasure of watching your financial world take shape, and the personal pride of achievement.

- If you're using a cloud-based program, although you have the convenience of being able to update and track on any web-enabled device, you will also be potentially exposing your personal financial data to unauthorized viewers.

You can do it all on pencil and ledger paper but you'll need to modify your methods of entry. Whatever method works for you will carry the day, so long as you encompass as many of the detailed information data points as I regularly track. You can tailor your method to make it as simple or as complex as you wish.

Start Simply

The basic starting goal is to be cognizant of exactly how much cash you have in your pocket, in your checking, in your savings, and in investments at any given time. If you track it you'll have an historical record, that you can go back and reflect upon, establish your income history and spending habits, and formulate ways to improve upon it. It also helps tremendously at tax time.

From that historical data you can then extrapolate into the future what you expect to have coming in and going out, cashwise. For example, I know that my electric utility bills increase in the winter and summer months, because of additional heating and air conditioning costs, and historically lower in the more temperate spring and fall months.

There's no magic to it, it's simple planning. And whatever works for you is what works for you. You just have to do it.

Not My Way Or The Highway

Before I even start populating any of my spreadsheets when setting up my annual tracking I will first create a separate simple sheet where I lay out all of my recurring income and bills, the days of the month they are usually due, and the approximate if not exact amounts due on those dates. This includes all income, including job income and contract income, then car payments, insurance, house mortgage/rent, utilities, credit card bills, anything that's recurring.

Knowing the total that I expect to have to pay out gives me a rudimentary budget that I can then work with. In the case of fluctuating payments, such as my electric bill, I start with an average amount for every month. When I go through the year's projections I'll adjust them seasonally, for the sake of closer realism (for example, seasonal fluctuations in utility bills).

I then create the working ledger sheets, one each for my checking accounts, and for my savings account. Finally, I create a sheet to track my retirement investments balances. Then finally a master summary with all subtotals that will give me an instantaneous snapshot of where I am and a reasonable projection of where I'm headed.

I only periodically update the investment account sheet since they are for the most part static investments. I'm not about to get sucked in and bogged down with the minutiae of stock market day-trading; I'm in it for the long haul, so I usually update those balances every week or so. I only track the overall portfolio value and not each individual security.

My main checking account is tied to my debit card. That's what I mainly use for purchases and most recurring payments. Starting with the main checking account ledger spreadsheet, and subsequently for every other ledger spreadsheet I then create a column for the date, one for the particular item/description, one for money coming in, one for money going out, and a running balance (simple credit/debit lines). I then populate the main checking account sheet, starting with January 1, then every row after with a sequential date, all the way through to December 31. I reference my master income and billing budgetary sheet that I have already set up to determine how much is expected or due on which day per month, and fill in every expected income and bill payment throughout the year on the date that it's respectively expected or due. And as the year progresses, I can modify any specific amount and instantly track how much I'll have at the end of the year, and most importantly, where it's distributed.

The beauty of it is that I can scroll through the spreadsheet and get a good personal financial picture, for both the past and projected for every single day of the year into the future. The end of year bottom line will change with every entry, of course; the end benefit is that you can get a snapshot of where you were, where you currently are, and where you'll be if nothing else changes for every single day of the year. It ends up at the end of the year as a good record of your budgeting and spending habits, and an invaluable reference when it comes to tax time.

The most important thing is, as with any tool, if you don't use it regularly it won't work for you. Doing it, keeping it up in daily chunks seems to work out fine.

See the fictional sample below:

	A	B	C	D	E
1					
2		**SAMPLE**			
3	Date	Item/Description	In	Out	Balance
4					
5	1/1	Beginning Balance	$1,765.43		$1,765.43
6	1/1	House Payment		$1,100.00	$665.43
7	1/2	Credit card bill		$150.00	$515.43
8	1/3	Paycheck	$1,200.00		$1,715.43
9	1/3	to Savings		$100.00	$1,615.43
10	1/3	Cash allowance		$100.00	$1,515.43
11	1/3	Groceries allowance		$100.00	$1,415.43
12	1/5	Car payment		$375.00	$1,040.43
13	1/10	Cable Bill		$160.00	$880.43
14	1/10	Telephone bill		$105.00	$775.43
15	1/10	Electric bill (avg)		$175.00	$600.43
16	1/10	Paycheck	$1,200.00		$1,800.43
17	1/10	to Savings		$100.00	$1,700.43
18	1/10	Cash allowance		$100.00	$1,600.43
19	1/10	Groceries allowance		$100.00	$1,500.43

This is how I might start the year out, carried through every day of the entire coming year.

This may take a little deep reading to grasp, but in practice it's simpler than it seems. I'll take you step by step through it. It's a slow read and might take a little time to grasp. If you invest the time to understand each step, at the very minimum you'll grasp the concepts of what needs to be done regularly, even if you don't implement this specific method. It'll at least bring to a point the awareness you'll need to have in order to begin being headed in the right financial direction, no matter which method you use.

I would, however, strongly suggest that you don't simply try to keep all of this in your head. The old expression is true: A dull pencil is sharper than the sharpest mind.

Anytime there are multiple entries on any particular day additional rows for that date will need to be added. For example, I have three bills that are due on the 10th of each month. So I copy the 10th to three lines for each month, expanding the spreadsheet by 24 extra lines for the year (the original 10th, plus the two additional entries for the 10th). For the 10th of each month I list the item in the item/description column, the amount of the anticipated income in the "In" column and the anticipated expenditures in the "Out" column. I keep a running balance of what's left by entering a formula on a "Balance" line including the ending balance from the previous line, plus the amount in the "In" cell, and minus the amount in the "Out" cell for that line. Once that formula is in place you can copy that formula to every cell thereafter. For example, in the example above the Balance shown in cell E8 contains the formula "=E7+C8-D8." That is, it takes the previous balance, and adds any amount that comes in and subtracts any amounts which may have been paid out. Copy and past that in every balance cell for the year, it will automatically adjust to the proper rows.

Note too in the above example that immediately after payday, I set aside savings and discretionary items. I color code the amount that I transfer to my savings account in light blue and light orange for the discretionary Cash and Groceries allowances. Once they have been set aside I'll color-code them the medium green to indicate that they've been dealt with. So I have $100 in the Groceries allowance, and $100 for pocket money. If I spend more than that I'll need to account for it in my spreadsheets by adding lines. On the other hand, if during the next pay period I have spending money left over, say $40, I'll replace the $60 spent, and transfer the money I don't take for pocket money into my savings.

As I said earlier, it's a way of tricking yourself into saving more money.

In a savings account. Where you don't touch it.

Sometimes we can't help but go over budget on food allowances, but we must be steadfast with our spending money and not just overspend and account for it on our spreadsheets; that defeats the whole purpose altogether.

4					
5	1/1	Beginning Balance	$1,765.43		$1,765.43
6	1/1	House Payment		$1,100.00	$665.43
7	1/2	Credit card bill		$150.00	$515.43
8	1/3	Paycheck	$1,200.00		$1,715.43

I have found it beneficial to use color coding on the spreadsheet cells to keep track of what has been paid and cleared. Any format you can understand and is pertinent to your needs is fine. I change the background color of the cell for a visual reference, and use a variety of cells to show a variety of applications. For the example above, on the 2nd of January, before I get paid, I use pale yellow on each Date cell to indicate that I've dealt with the item. On business-related tax-deduction items I change the Date cell to a medium orange color (not shown in the above example) -- this aids tremendously at tax time. The beginning balance is accounted for in checking, so it gets a medium green color. I wrote a check for the House Payment, which is highlighted in yellow, until it clears the bank. The credit card bill was paid on the 2nd, but has not yet cleared the bank, so it gets a darker green color. When the check and the online payments clear, then I will change the background color to the cleared medium green color.

I try to pay electronically wherever possible; it cuts down on check printing charges. Consequently, I only write a few checks per month. Whenever I have an outstanding check, I note it by giving it a bright yellow background. Once the check clears the bank, the background color then gets changed to the medium green.

Again, this is what works for me. Any recurring specialty items can be color-coded so you can see at a glance what has cleared. In the above example, at the end of the day on the 2nd, my checking account will still show the $1,763.45 balance, but I know I've paid two bills by two different methods which have not yet cleared the bank. My bank says the $1,700 plus balance, but I know that I only actually have $515.43 to work with in my checking account.

Keeping up with the daily reporting, then, becomes largely one of color code changing and maybe adding and adjusting additional lines for unscheduled entries, like, say, if I use my bank debit card to gas up the car, I would add a line.

If you're curious about any specific items in your tracking, you can always note it with your own custom color coding or formatting. For example, when my balances in my spreadsheet jibe with my bank statements, I'll change the date cell to a bold font. This lets me know that my accounts are squared at least from that date. It flags a starting point for me when the two balances get out of sync.

12 - Conclusion

Be Committed

As has been stressed many times in this book, in order to begin to achieve financial independence, it is absolutely essential for you to be committed to being mindful of your money. All the time, not just occasionally. Like dogs, they need to be confined to a pen until they have learned to not stray from home. You have to continually watch out for them until they're trained (that is, you have the discipline down pat) to stay in their own yard.

Even when they're trained, you still need to be vigilant and regularly do a head-count to make sure they're all present and accounted for. The wolves can sneak in during the night time if you're not vigilant. During the good times are especially those when you need to be wary and extremely of falling into complacency. Don't ever let your guard down.

Make it a habit. It'll pay off for you. Do it long enough, and it really doesn't take that long, and after a short while it'll become just an automatic thing that you do. You've changed your behavior to include a future of prosperity, and this is perhaps the most important lesson of all. Once you've adopted these changes into your personal culture, it will be automatic, something that is simply second nature to you.

Turn The Negative Around

The entire thrust of this book is to take the book title, which has been named as such in contrast to the ideal, because it is a phrase I've heard and used all too many times. I even used to hear it frequently from my own children. Over time, they've begun to realize that their struggles in life can be so much easier to bear with a comfortable cushion under them, and thankfully have begun to implement the principles contained herein.

Delete the entire phrase from your vocabulary. Turn it around to what the implied meaning actually is…"I **Can** Afford To Save Money." You do it by simply applying the age-old tenet, "Pay Yourself First." Don't worry, you'll figure out a magical way to make do with what's left over after that.

Gear Yourself To Delayed Gratification

Madison Avenue, Wall Street, and the Joneses will tell you that instant gratification rules the day. They'll hammer into you that you should and can be able to have everything and anything you want, up to the limits of your social strata's particular buying power, and then plus a little more. Just enough to keep you in a bind.

Remember, the money changers make all of the money by keeping you in debt and getting a large share of your money as interest on using theirs. Simply understanding that singular concept should be sufficient to open your eyes as to the real nature of money.

Our entire culture has been based upon an instant

gratification model. We all tend to think we need much more than we actually do, because we've been inundated with overt and covert subliminal messages telling us just that. Sure, it's nice to have nice things, and they make it easy for us to overextend ourselves. That's when we've traded our personal freedoms for a comfort that is subject to the whims of others.

And it isn't really your fault. It's completely societal programming that uses very subtle and subliminal cues to convince you that you need more stuff. The truth is you don't. It's the old psychological sleight of hand, masterfully using a barrage of misdirection that is specifically calculated for you to keep your eyes off of the ball. Your prosperity ball.

This does not mean that you will need to deny yourself every bit of life's simple pleasures, but the fact is you have to be completely honest with yourself about whether or not you actually need something, or just want something. Consider trying delayed gratification instead of the just-add-water instant style. It works for brewed coffee versus instant, why not for you?

Be wise about it. Watch the other hand while Madison Avenue and the Joneses are working on you. It's sticking your cash into its own pockets.

Watch The Big Picture, Some Parting Thoughts

Look at the bigger picture. By tying yourself up in a knot of debt, you'll incur more stress just trying to figure out how to pay for the interest on all of the extra stuff you have that you don't have the time to enjoy.

Neither is it so focused on placing the love of your money above all else in your life. Unless your goal in life is to be able to afford the biggest tombstone in the cemetery.

The idea of this book is to become financially stabilized enough so that you can properly enjoy all aspects of your life, without paying unnecessarily for it. To have the freedom, safety, and personal security to not have to worry later on in life.

It's important to work hard in life, to be sure. But also just as important is to work smart in your life. This book gives you suggestions for the myriad pathways to financial freedom. If you only implement a few of these suggestions into your life, it will put you well ahead of the game.

You actually can have nice things. But you need to purpose to do it.

– **END** --

ABOUT THE AUTHOR

R. Lee Townsend is a writer, musician, amateur radio operator, airplane pilot, educator, paranormal researcher, philanthropist, music producer and engineer. With such a wide variety of interests and life experiences he has many stories to tell. Raised in Baltimore MD as the son of an attorney and grandson of a spy, his books are likewise written on a wide variety of topics, but his storytelling style is both simultaneously informal and informative; he loves words.

www.ingramcontent.com/pod-product-compliance
Lightning Source LLC
Chambersburg PA
CBHW070444220526
45466CB00004B/1764